COOLSCULPTING AND CRYOLIPOLYSIS FOR BEGINNERS

Effective Treatment Tips For Rapid Fat Reduction And Non-Invasive Body Techniques

DR SAWYER DIEGO

Copyright © [2024] by [Dr. .Sawyer Diego]. All rights reserved.

Except for brief quotations included in critical reviews and certain other noncommercial uses allowed by copyright law, no part of this publication may be reproduced, distributed, or transmitted in any form or by any means, including photocopying, recording, or other electronic or mechanical methods, without the publisher's prior written permission.

DISCLAMER

Nothing in this book should be interpreted as medical advice; it is meant exclusively for educational reasons. Regarding their specific health issues and treatment options, readers are urged to speak with licensed healthcare professionals. The publisher and author disclaim all liability for any errors or omissions in the material provided, as well as for any negative effects that may arise from using or abusing the information. Although every attempt has been taken to guarantee that the material in this book is correct as of the date of publishing, new research may have superseded some of the content because medical knowledge is always changing. It is recommended that readers confirm the most recent medical recommendations and guidelines. The reader of this book undertakes to release the author and publisher from any claims or liabilities resulting from the use of this information, and understands and accepts the inherent risks connected with healthcare decisions.

TABLE OF CONTENTS

CHAPTER ONE 13
   COOLSCULPTING AND CRYOLIPOLYSIS OVERVIEW 13
      WHAT IS CRYOLIPOLYSIS AND COOLSCULPTING? 13
      COOLSCULPTING'S ADVANTAGES FOR BODY CONTOURING 15
      SAFETY ASPECTS AND EFFICIENCY..16
      COMPREHENDING THE PROCESS TIMETABLE 18
      WAYS TO GET READY FOR YOUR COOLSCULPTING..........................20

CHAPTER TWO 23
   COMPREHENDING COOLSCULPTING..23
      HOW TO USE COOLSCULPTING 23
      THE SCIENCE OF CRYOLIPOLYSIS 24
      TARGETED TREATMENT AREAS 25
      NORMAL OUTCOMES AND ANTICIPATIONS......................................26
      BENEFITS COMPARED TO CONVENTIONAL LIPOSUCTION 27

CHAPTER THREE 29
   SELECTING THE APPROPRIATE SUPPLIER 29
      LOOKING UP ELIGIBLE CLINICS 29
      SPEAKING WITH AN EXPERT..30
      ASSESSING REHABILITATION PROGRAMS 31
      EXAMINING PATIENT RETESTS 32
      THINGS TO CONSIDER BEFORE INVESTING 33

CHAPTER FOUR 35
   GETTING READY FOR YOUR COOLSCULPTING TREATMENT..................35
      PRE-PROCEDURE INSTRUCTIONS 35

    WHAT TO PUT ON FOR THE DAY OF TREATMENT 36

    CONTROLLING EXPECTATIONS 37

    TIPS FOR MENTAL PREPARATION 38

    COMMONLY HELD MYTHS DISPELLED 39

CHAPTER FIVE 41

  THROUGHOUT YOUR COOLSCULPTING APPOINTMENT 41

    OVERVIEW OF THE STEP-BY-STEP PROCEDURE 41

    COMFORT AND SENSITIVITY LEVELS 42

    THE LENGTH OF EVERY THERAPY CYCLE 43

    KNOWING ABOUT COOLING PANELS 44

    THINGS TO DO WHILE RECEIVING TREATMENT 45

CHAPTER SIX 47

  AFTER CARE AND RECUPERATION 47

    QUICK AFTERCARE GUIDELINES 47

    HANDLING TRANSIENT SIDE EFFECTS 48

    RETURNING TO REGULAR ACTIVITIES 49

    MAINTENANCE OF LONG-TERM RESULTS 50

    ADDITIONAL VISITS AND EVALUATIONS 51

CHAPTER SEVEN 53

  FAQS & FREQUENTLY ASKED QUESTIONS 53

    DOES COOLSCULPTING CAUSE PAIN? 53

    EXIST ANY HAZARDS CONCERNED? 54

    HOW MANY APPOINTMENTS ARE REQUIRED? 55

    CAN SEVERAL AREAS BE TREATED WITH COOLSCULPTING? 57

    WHAT KIND OF OUTCOMES SHOULD I EXPECT? 58

CHAPTER EIGHT 61

IMPROVING OUTCOMES WITH LIFESTYLE MODIFICATIONS 61

THE SIGNIFICANCE OF EATING WELL 61
INCLUDING FREQUENT EXERCISE 62
TIPS FOR HYDRATION AND SKIN CARE 64
MENTAL HEALTH AND PERCEPTION OF BODY 65
LONG-TERM WEIGHT LOSS TECHNIQUES 67

CHAPTER NINE 69

FURTHER USES FOR COOLSCULPTING 69

COOLSCULPTING SUITABLE FOR VARIOUS BODY SHAPES 69
COMBINING CERTAIN PROCEDURES WITH OTHER 70
SPECIFICALLY ADDRESSING FAT DEPOSITS 72
INNOVATIONS IN NON-SURGICAL BODY CONTOURING 73
EXAMINING POTENTIAL ADVANCES IN CRYOLIPOLYSIS 74

CHAPTER TEN 77

COST FACTORS AND AVAILABLE FINANCING 77

COMPREHENDING PRICING STRUCTURES 77
VIEWS ON INSURANCE COVERAGE 78
PLANS FOR FINANCING AVAILABLE 79
COMPARING THE PRICE OF CONVENTIONAL LIPOSUCTION 80
TIPS FOR BUDGETING TOWARD AFFORDABILITY 81

CHAPTER ELEVEN 83

TEACHING PEOPLE ABOUT COOLSCULPTING 83

PROMOTING A POSITIVE ATTITUDE 83
DESCRIBE YOUR OWN EXPERIENCE 85

SOURCES FOR ADDITIONAL READING 86

RAISING AWARENESS IN YOUR NEIGHBORHOOD 88

HELPING OTHERS WITH THEIR COOLSCULPTING EXPERIENCES.........90

ABOUT THE BOOK

For those interested in non-invasive body contouring procedures such as CoolSculpting, the book "CoolSculpting and Cryolipolysis for Beginners" is a must-have resource. It seeks to make cryo lipolysis approachable and comprehensible for novices by demystifying the procedure and its advantages of.

Cryolipolysis and CoolSculpting are cutting-edge non-surgical methods for eliminating hard-to-remove fat deposits. It is vital for anyone seeking to properly achieve targeted fat reduction to comprehend the workings of these strategies. The book makes clear how targeted chilling can specifically target fat cells while sparing surrounding tissue by elucidating the chemistry behind cryolipolysis.

In any cosmetic operation, safety and efficacy are of utmost importance. This book goes into great detail regarding these topics, including the safety profile of the procedure and what kind of outcomes candidates should reasonably expect.

It also discusses the benefits of CoolSculpting over conventional liposuction, highlighting its minimal recovery time and non-invasive nature.

Selecting the appropriate supplier is essential to having CoolSculpting. The book walks readers through the process of finding accredited facilities, speaking with experts, and assessing treatment programs. It also offers advice on how to evaluate patient endorsements and what crucial inquiries to make before beginning treatment.

There is more to getting ready for a CoolSculpting treatment than just turning up. The book covers expectations management, what to anticipate in the session, and pre-procedure guidelines. It dispels myths that are frequently held and provides advice on mental readiness to guarantee a good experience.

For peace of mind throughout the CoolSculpting session, it is important to comprehend the overview of the step-by-step method and the sensations to be anticipated.

The book includes information on the length of each treatment cycle, the function of cooling panels, and comfortable activities to pass the time.

Maintaining results requires both recuperation and post-treatment care. To guarantee a seamless recuperation process, guidelines for immediate aftercare, handling transient side effects, and returning to regular activities are all addressed. To maximize results, emphasis is placed on maintaining long-term results and the significance of lifestyle modifications including frequent exercise and a nutritious diet.

Advanced uses of CoolSculpting are examined, such as its suitability for various body types, how well it works in conjunction with other procedures, and new developments in non-surgical body sculpting. Future innovations in cryolipolysis are also covered in the book, along with economic issues and possible advances.

Building a supportive network can be achieved by educating others about CoolSculpting and supporting body positivity. To enable readers to share their stories and encourage others on their CoolSculpting journeys, the book provides resources for additional reading and advice on raising awareness.

CHAPTER ONE

COOLSCULPTING AND CRYOLIPOLYSIS OVERVIEW

WHAT IS CRYOLIPOLYSIS AND COOLSCULPTING?

Cryolipolysis, another name for CoolSculpting, is a non-invasive cosmetic surgery used to target troublesome fat deposits in different parts of the body. It functions on the premise that fat cells are more sensitive to low temperatures than the tissues around them. A specialized device is utilized during a CoolSculpting session to target areas with excess fat. Without endangering the skin, the device uses controlled refrigeration to freeze the fat cells beneath the surface. The frozen fat cells eventually solidify and die, at which point the lymphatic system naturally removes them from the body.

Because it can target and remove fat bulges that resist diet and exercise, this therapy is well-liked. It is frequently applied to regions like the thighs, abdomen, love handles, and under the chin. When it comes to helping healthy people achieve better body shapes without requiring surgery or recovery time, CoolSculpting is thought to be both safe and effective. As the body gradually breaks down the removed fat cells, the results usually take a few weeks to months to become apparent.

Before undergoing CoolSculpting, patients usually speak with a certified professional to find out if they are a good fit based on their medical background and desired appearance.

Many people seeking non-surgical body reshaping treatments with low risks and short recovery times find the process appealing because it doesn't involve surgery. Gaining knowledge about CoolSculpting's advantages and how it operates can empower those looking for a non-invasive solution to tone their bodies and boost their self-esteem.

COOLSCULPTING'S ADVANTAGES FOR BODY CONTOURING

For those seeking non-surgical body reshaping, CoolSculpting provides several advantages. Its non-invasive nature, which eliminates the need for incisions and anesthesia, is one of its main benefits. As a result, patients can resume their regular activities right away following treatment, lowering the dangers connected with surgical treatments and eliminating the need for recovery time.

Particularly addressing localized fat deposits, the targeted cooling technology helps to smooth and contour areas that are frequently difficult to reach with diet and exercise alone.

The progressive and natural-looking outcomes of CoolSculpting are yet another important advantage. Patients usually see a progressive decrease in fat bulges over time as the treated fat cells are eventually removed from the body. This organic process produces a more subtle improvement that enhances the body's natural features without causing abrupt changes that are occasionally linked to surgical operations. CoolSculpting procedures are also adaptable and can be customized to fit a variety of body types, giving many people looking for body sculpting options a personalized alternative.

Additionally, patients usually tolerate CoolSculpting well and experience little side effects. The treated area may have some transient side effects, such as redness, swelling, or numbness, which usually go away on their own in a few days to weeks. Because of this, it's a good option for people who want to improve their looks through a process that consistently produces excellent outcomes and high patient satisfaction. People can decide whether CoolSculpting is the best solution for their body-reshaping goals by being aware of these benefits.

SAFETY ASPECTS AND EFFICIENCY

For suitable people, CoolSculpting is thought to be a safe and efficient procedure for decreasing localized fat deposits. The FDA has approved the treatment, which uses controlled cooling technology to target fat cells under the skin without endangering other tissues. In authorized medical facilities, clinical research and patient reviews typically confirm its safety profile when carried out by qualified personnel.

The precise area of the body being treated, the quantity of fat being treated, and the patient's compliance with post-procedure instructions are some of the unique aspects that affect how effective CoolSculpting is.

Although the effects are modest and can take a few weeks to show up, many patients eventually report better body shapes and a discernible decrease in bulging fat. Patients must speak with a licensed professional who can determine whether they are a good candidate for the surgery and have reasonable expectations regarding the results of CoolSculpting.

When done by a certified specialist, CoolSculpting usually has very little risk in terms of safety.

Temporary numbness, redness, swelling, or bruises at the treatment site are common side effects that usually go away on their own. Paradoxical adipose hyperplasia (PAH), an uncommon syndrome in which fat cells in the treated area grow rather than shrink, is one of the rare but potentially serious consequences. But this is rare—less than 1% of cases experience this. People can make more informed judgments about using CoolSculpting for body sculpting if they are aware of these safety concerns.

COMPREHENDING THE PROCESS TIMETABLE

Usually, a consultation is held before the CoolSculpting operation to evaluate the patient's objectives and choose the best course of action. The targeted region is marked and a gel pad is used to protect the skin during the actual treatment session. Next, the CoolSculpting applicator is placed over the treatment region, freezing the fat cells beneath the skin with regulated cooling.

Depending on the size and quantity of regions being treated, each treatment session might run anywhere from 35 minutes to an hour per area. To get the best results, it could be advised to have multiple sessions, particularly for larger or more resistant fat deposits. Patients don't need to take time off after the operation because CoolSculpting doesn't involve any incisions or anesthesia.

The body breaks down the frozen fat cells over the next few weeks to months, which causes the treated areas' fat bulges to gradually disappear. Within a few weeks, patients usually start to experience improvements, which last for several months until the body finishes the removal process. It may be necessary to plan routine follow-up consultations to assess progress and assess whether further treatments are required to reach the intended results.

Comprehending the CoolSculpting timeframe might aid patients in getting ready for the treatment and its aftermath. A healthy lifestyle and adherence to the prescribed treatment plan can help people achieve the best possible outcomes and long-lasting body reshaping.

WAYS TO GET READY FOR YOUR COOLSCULPTING APPOINTMENT

To guarantee the best possible outcomes and seamless recuperation, there are a few preparations involved in getting ready for a CoolSculpting treatment. Patients should make an appointment for a consultation with a qualified provider before the procedure to go over their problems, medical history, and cosmetic goals.

The practitioner will determine whether CoolSculpting is appropriate based on the patient's unique traits and expectations during this consultation.

It's crucial to keep your weight steady before the session by eating a balanced diet and getting frequent exercise. CoolSculpting is meant to be used as a technique to target fat deposits that resist lifestyle changes rather than as a weight reduction aid.

Recuperation after therapy and general skin health can also be aided by drinking less alcohol and being hydrated.

Patients should dress comfortably so that they can easily enter the treatment area on the day of the operation. Preventing bruising by abstaining from anti-inflammatory drugs like ibuprofen or aspirin before treatment can help reduce the chance of bruises. Additionally, if necessary, the practitioner may provide special recommendations, such as shaving the treatment region, to guarantee the best possible contact between the CoolSculpting applicator and the skin.

As CoolSculpting doesn't require any downtime, patients may usually get back to their regular activities right away after the treatment. Some minor side effects, such as transient redness or numbness, are possible but normally go away in a few days on their own. Optimizing results can be achieved by adhering to the post-procedure instructions given by the practitioner, which may include massaging the treated area gently and limiting sun exposure.

To guarantee a good treatment experience and satisfying results, properly preparing for a CoolSculpting session includes knowing the process, keeping general health, and adhering to pre-session instructions.

CHAPTER TWO
COMPREHENDING COOLSCULPTING
HOW TO USE COOLSCULPTING

CoolSculpting is a non-invasive technique that uses controlled cooling technology to remove fat deposits in specific areas of the body. The method relies on the freezing of fat cells with little damage to the surrounding tissues, a process known as cryolipolysis. A specialized applicator is put to the desired location during a CoolSculpting session, and it precisely distributes chilling to freeze the fat cells beneath the skin's surface.

The normal process of cell death known as apoptosis occurs in the frozen fat cells. The lymphatic system of the body gradually gets rid of these dead fat cells. Fat in the treated area decreases as a result of this gradual removal process; this reduction is usually seen a few weeks to a few months after treatment. CoolSculpting works especially well for areas of fat that don't respond well to diet or exercise.

THE SCIENCE OF CRYOLIPOLYSIS

The method of specifically targeting and freezing fat cells—known as cryolipolysis—is the basis of CoolSculpting's scientific basis. When it comes to freezing temperatures, fat cells are more vulnerable than surrounding tissues such as muscles, skin, and nerves.

During CoolSculpting, regulated cooling promotes a process in which fat cells solidify and finally die off without endangering healthy cells.

The body's natural metabolic systems begin to work after the fat cells solidify, progressively eliminating them. The treated area gets thinner over the ensuing weeks and months as the fat cells are naturally broken down and eliminated by the lymphatic system. Without requiring surgery, this scientific method guarantees that fat removal happens in a targeted and controlled manner, improving contours noticeably.

TARGETED TREATMENT AREAS

CoolSculpting works well for treating several body parts where accumulated fat tends to be recalcitrant. The abdomen, thighs, upper arms, bra fat area, love handles (flanks), and double chin are common target areas.

These areas are perfect candidates for CoolSculpting's fat-freezing technology since they are usually resistant to diet and exercise. Every treatment session is customized to target particular problem areas according to each patient's goals and body type.

The adaptability of CoolSculpting applicators makes it possible to precisely target various body areas, guaranteeing that every treatment is tailored to produce the best possible outcomes. CoolSculpting is a non-surgical way to sculpt the body in the areas that most irritate people, whether it be slimming down thighs or decreasing belly bulges.

NORMAL OUTCOMES AND ANTICIPATIONS

Although individual results from CoolSculpting treatments vary, most people start to notice improvements a few weeks after the procedure. Gradual fat reduction becomes apparent when the body naturally gets rid of the treated fat cells; the best benefits usually appear in two to three months. A more sculpted appearance is achieved for many people by a noticeable increase in body contours and a decrease in fat bulges.

It's crucial to understand that CoolSculpting is a body sculpting technique rather than a weight loss medication.

The ideal individuals are close to their goal weight but have stubborn fat in particular places that they would like to lose. A balanced diet, frequent exercise, and a healthy lifestyle can help people get the most out of and stay longer with CoolSculpting procedures.

BENEFITS COMPARED TO CONVENTIONAL LIPOSUCTION

Compared to traditional liposuction, CoolSculpting has several benefits, chief among them being its non-invasive technique for targeted fat reduction. For many people,

CoolSculpting is a safer and more comfortable option than liposuction because it doesn't require incisions or anesthesia, unlike liposuction, which requires surgery and recovery time. There is a lower chance of complications and a faster healing period when there are no surgical incisions.

Furthermore, unlike standard liposuction, CoolSculpting enables precise targeting of fat cells without endangering nearby tissues. CoolSculpting's gradual fat reduction process also yields natural-looking results that change over time, unlike liposuction, which usually produces more immediate but occasionally inconsistent results.

CHAPTER THREE
SELECTING THE APPROPRIATE SUPPLIER
LOOKING UP ELIGIBLE CLINICS

The first important step in exploring the realm of cryolipolysis and CoolSculpting is finding accredited clinics. Start by using web tools to find clinics that specialize in these procedures, such as review sites and medical directories. Seek out businesses that have received great reviews from customers and high ratings, as these points to a history of effective treatments. It is imperative to confirm the qualifications of professionals and make sure they are certified to perform cryolipolysis and CoolSculpting.

Take into account the clinic's years of expertise in providing aesthetic treatments as well as its general reputation. An established clinic is usually an indication of competence and dependability when it comes to performing these non-invasive procedures for fat reduction.

Examine the clinic's amenities and technological setup to make sure the newest models are being used for the best outcomes and patient comfort.

Finally, get in touch with the clinic directly to find out whether a consultation is available and to talk about any specific worries you may have about cryolipolysis and CoolSculpting. By choosing a respectable facility with the resources to produce safe and efficient results, this initial research stage establishes the groundwork for a fruitful therapeutic journey.

SPEAKING WITH AN EXPERT

After you've narrowed down your list of possible clinics, the next important step is to make appointments with CoolSculpting and cryolipolysis specialists. You will be able to discuss your aesthetic objectives and determine whether the treatment is right for you during these visits.

A trained professional will perform a comprehensive evaluation of your target regions and go over the anticipated results of cryolipolysis or CoolSculpting. They will go into great depth about the course of treatment, outlining what to anticipate before, during, and following each session.

Asking precise questions regarding recovery durations, possible side effects, and any alternative therapies that might be appropriate for your goals is also a great idea during consultations. Before proceeding with treatment, use this chance to assess the specialist's communication style and make sure you are at ease and confident in their knowledge.

ASSESSING REHABILITATION PROGRAMS

The next step is to assess suggested CoolSculpting or cryolipolysis treatment regimens after speaking with specialists. Every treatment plan needs to be customized according to your particular body type and desired results.

The expert will describe how many sessions are needed to get the best outcomes and how long it should go between sessions. They will go over the areas that need to be addressed and give you an estimated time frame for when body contouring will start to show results.

If you've spoken with multiple clinics, it's critical to compare treatment plans from each during this evaluation period.

Take into account elements like price, length of treatment, and degree of customization provided by each plan. Select a course of treatment that will best help you achieve your aesthetic objectives while staying within your means and timetable.

EXAMINING PATIENT RETESTS

Examine patient endorsements and success stories from the facility you are considering before deciding to undergo CoolSculpting or cryolipolysis treatment. Sincere patient testimonials offer insightful information about the general patient experience, therapeutic outcomes, and satisfaction levels.

Seek reviews that touch on particular topics, such as the comfort level during sessions, the staff's professionalism, and the efficacy of the treatment. Observe any reoccurring themes or issues brought up by several patients; this can provide a fair assessment of what to anticipate.

Furthermore, some clinics might display before and after pictures of past cryolipolysis or CoolSculpting patients. These illustrations can help you picture the treatment's transformational impacts and offer you a realistic sneak peek at the possible results.

THINGS TO CONSIDER BEFORE INVESTING

Make a list of important questions for your final visit with the specialist before deciding to proceed with CoolSculpting or cryolipolysis. These queries ought to answer any residual worries or doubts you might have regarding the process.

Find out about the specialist's track record of handling situations comparable to yours and how successful they are at getting the results you want. Ask about the particular dangers involved in cryolipolysis or CoolSculpting, and what precautions are taken to reduce these risks while undergoing treatment.

Additionally, include information on the treatment's cost, including any possible extra charges for maintenance or follow-up visits. Recognize the clinic's cancellation and rescheduling policies to ensure that you have flexibility in case of unanticipated events.

You may empower yourself to make confident judgments about moving forward with cryolipolysis or CoolSculpting by asking detailed and knowledgeable questions. By being proactive, you can be sure that you are ready for the treatment process and that you will have a great time working with your selected facility.

CHAPTER FOUR

GETTING READY FOR YOUR COOLSCULPTING TREATMENT

PRE-PROCEDURE INSTRUCTIONS

To get the best results from your CoolSculpting session, it's important to adhere to a few pre-procedure instructions. First, discuss your objectives and determine if you're a good candidate for CoolSculpting with your provider. They could advise taking precautions like avoiding vitamins and anti-inflammatory drugs that raise the risk of bleeding. It's important to stay hydrated; consuming lots of water in the days before your session will aid in your body's faster removal of fat cells after treatment.

Furthermore, keep your weight steady before your visit because large weight swings may have an impact on the result. Make sure you have healthy, unbroken skin in the treatment region that is free of sunburn or rashes. Lastly, to allay any worries and guarantee that you show up for your session well-informed and prepared, familiarize yourself with the procedure specifics supplied by your provider.

WHAT TO PUT ON FOR THE DAY OF TREATMENT

The efficiency of the process and your level of comfort can both be greatly impacted by what you wear on the day of your CoolSculpting treatment. Choose loose, cozy attire that will make it simple to enter the therapy area. Many patients dress in loose-fitting skirts, shirts, and slacks that are easy to draw up or down to suit the area being treated.

After the treatment, stay away from wearing tight clothes or undergarments that could compress the treated area as this could impede the natural cooling process and have an impact on your outcomes. Your CoolSculpting provider can make specific clothing recommendations based on the regions being treated and how comfortable you want the procedure to be if you're not sure what to wear. You can guarantee a seamless and stress-free experience on the day of your CoolSculpting session by dressing properly and appropriately.

CONTROLLING EXPECTATIONS

When having CoolSculpting therapy, it's important to control your expectations. Although it's a really powerful way to lose fat that won't go away, it's vital to realize that the effects might not show up right away. Notable results usually appear in a few weeks to months when your body gets rid of the treated fat cells on its own.

It's also critical to understand that CoolSculpting is a body sculpting treatment rather than a weight-loss operation. It targets particular places where, despite diet and exercise regimens, fat tends to collect. To match expectations with what CoolSculpting can accomplish for you, talk about reasonable goals with your provider during the consultation. You may approach your treatment with patience and confidence if you know exactly how it will work and when it will happen.

TIPS FOR MENTAL PREPARATION

A favorable experience with CoolSculpting can be greatly enhanced by psychologically preparing for the procedure. To reduce anxiety and boost confidence, start by learning about the treatment and its advantages. Imagine the results you want to see, emphasizing how the procedure will improve the shape of your body and your entire look.

To help you remain composed throughout the process, try some relaxation techniques like deep breathing or meditation. To allay any residual fears, discuss any worries or inquiries you may have with your CoolSculpting provider in advance. Assist yourself by surrounding yourself with family or friends who will be there for you every step of the way. You may go into your CoolSculpting treatment day with a positive outlook and be ready to get the results you want by mentally preparing for the procedure.

COMMONLY HELD MYTHS DISPELLED

It will be easier for you to make decisions about your treatment if you know the facts about the most widespread misunderstandings around CoolSculpting. A common misperception is that CoolSculpting may replace weight reduction. In actuality, it's made to contour particular places, and it works best for people who suffer from stubborn fat pockets and are nearing their target weight.

There is also a myth that CoolSculpting causes weight loss to happen right away. Although the body gradually reduces fat as it metabolizes treated fat cells, appreciable effects usually take weeks to months to show.

Furthermore, some people could be under the false impression that CoolSculpting is uncomfortable or requires a lot of downtime. Nonetheless, the majorities of patients have only minor discomfort throughout the process and can quickly return to their regular activities.

It's critical to refute the notion that CoolSculpting produces uneven results or contours that don't seem natural. CoolSculpting can produce body contouring effects that are smooth and natural-looking when done by a trained practitioner. You can approach your CoolSculpting procedure with reasonable expectations and trust in its efficacy if you are aware of these disproven myths.

CHAPTER FIVE

THROUGHOUT YOUR COOLSCULPTING APPOINTMENT

OVERVIEW OF THE STEP-BY-STEP PROCEDURE

Gaining confidence and comfort throughout your CoolSculpting treatment depends on your ability to follow the detailed instructions. Usually, the session starts with a consultation during which a qualified practitioner discusses your objectives and the areas that need to be treated. When you're prepared to continue, a treatment bed will be used to comfortably position you. After that, the desired region will be marked and ready for the applicator to be placed.

After that, the specified area is treated using the CoolSculpting applicator. A small suction may be felt as the applicator sticks to your skin. Gradually freezing the skin's surface is intended to target and freeze fat cells below the surface without damaging surrounding tissues.

You could initially feel extremely cold throughout the treatment, but these feelings usually go away as the area numbs.

You can unwind, read, or even use your laptop throughout a session as the treatment goes on. Depending on the particular applicator and the area being treated, each cycle has a different duration. The applicator is taken out after the designated amount of time, and a quick massage of the treated area may be applied to promote fat breakdown. After that, you can get back to your regular activities right away because CoolSculpting is a non-invasive process that doesn't need any recovery time.

COMFORT AND SENSITIVITY LEVELS

It's easier to control expectations and guarantee a more comfortable procedure when one is aware of the feelings and comfort levels during CoolSculpting. The applicator may cause you to first experience severe cold and pulling sensations as it drags the targeted tissue into the device.

This sensation quickly goes away because the cooling action on the skin and underlying fat cells causes the area to become numb.

Many patients report feeling comfortable enough to partake in mild activities like reading, listening to music, or checking emails from work throughout treatment. After treatment, some people may have brief symptoms of tingling, stinging, or moderate cramping as the region warms up. These feelings are common and usually go away a few minutes to several hours following the session.

It's best to dress comfortably and loosely for your CoolSculpting treatment to maximize comfort. If you are uncomfortable, be honest with your practitioner so that changes can be made to ensure that your treatment is comfortable and meets your needs.

THE LENGTH OF EVERY THERAPY CYCLE

The size and quantity of regions being treated determine how long each CoolSculpting treatment cycle lasts. Sessions often run between thirty-five and an hour depending on the type of treatment. Longer sessions could be necessary to get the best effects in larger or more regions.

Based on your unique objectives and the areas you want to target, your practitioner will suggest a customized treatment plan at your initial appointment. The projected amount of time required for each session to achieve the targeted fat loss will be specified in this plan.

Knowing how long each treatment cycle lasts will help you adjust your schedule. Because CoolSculpting requires little downtime, many patients find it simple to schedule sessions during lunch breaks or work them into their regular schedule.

KNOWING ABOUT COOLING PANELS

CoolSculpting targets and freezes fat cells beneath the skin's surface using cooling panels. These panels are a component of the applicators that are made to fit different treatment regions in varied sizes and forms. The targeted fat cells are subjected to regulated cooling by the panels, which causes them to solidify and finally die off.

Every applicator is made with cooling panels that stick to the skin, providing accurate and efficient care. You can experience extreme cold at first, followed by numbness as the cooling effect sets in. This is all because of the panels. Your practitioner closely monitors this procedure to guarantee safe, regular fat loss that doesn't harm nearby tissues.

Most patients only feel a little discomfort once the first cold feeling wears off thanks to the cooling panels' ergonomic design, which makes for comfortable treatment sessions.

THINGS TO DO WHILE RECEIVING TREATMENT

You are free to do anything you want to comfortably pass the time during your CoolSculpting treatment. Many patients decide to use a laptop or mobile device to catch up on work, read a book, or listen to music as a way to unwind. CoolSculpting is non-invasive, so you can stay awake and conscious the entire time, which makes it easy to multitask or just relax.

To further improve relaxation, some patients choose to meditate or perform deep breathing techniques during their treatment sessions. To guarantee that the targeted area is not disturbed during CoolSculpting sessions, light activities that don't include a lot of movement or perspiration are preferable.

It's crucial to discuss any preferences or activities you want to partake in while therapy with your practitioner. To maximize the procedure's efficiency and make sure you have a stress-free, enjoyable experience overall, they might offer advice on placement and comfort. You may maximize your CoolSculpting session and easily get your desired body-shaping goals by selecting relaxing activities.

CHAPTER SIX
AFTER CARE AND RECUPERATION
QUICK AFTERCARE GUIDELINES

It's critical to adhere to the post-procedure recommendations promptly following CoolSculpting or cryolipolysis to maximize outcomes and reduce discomfort. It's common for the treated area to feel numb, bloated, or sensitive to touch right after treatment; these side effects usually go away in a few days. Use a cold compress on your skin occasionally to calm it and lessen swelling to control these effects. During the first several days following treatment, stay away from physically demanding activities and exposure of the treated area to extreme temperatures.

Drinking enough of water will help your body's natural healing process during this time. To aid in the removal of fat cells that are the focus of the operation, stay hydrated and abstain from alcohol. Sustain a nutrient-dense, well-balanced diet to promote healing and guarantee the best outcomes.

Observe any particular guidance on medication or extra care regimens given by your healthcare practitioner based on your personal needs. Following CoolSculpting or cryolipolysis, you can improve comfort and encourage efficient recovery by following these initial aftercare instructions.

HANDLING TRANSIENT SIDE EFFECTS

After cryo-lipolysis or CoolSculpting, transient side effects are typical but treatable with appropriate attention. It is common to feel tingling, itching, or numbness in the treated area; these symptoms usually go away on their own after a few weeks. Redness, swelling, or mild bruising are also possible but should go away with time. Refrain from rubbing or scratching the treated area, and do not apply cold packs or heating pads directly to the skin to reduce discomfort.

Acetaminophen is one type of over-the-counter pain medication that can aid with any discomfort. Before taking any post-treatment medicine, make sure you speak with your healthcare professional and follow the dosage directions. Dress comfortably and loosely to reduce pressure on the treated region and encourage recovery. Additionally, a little massage of the affected area may help to promote lymphatic drainage and lessen swelling. For individualized advice and comfort if you are worried about any side effects or how long they will last, get in touch with your healthcare professional.

RETURNING TO REGULAR ACTIVITIES

Following CoolSculpting or cryolipolysis, getting back into your routine requires a gradual return to physical activities while keeping an eye on your body's reaction. After treatment, you can usually resume modest activities right once, but to give your body time to heal completely, avoid strenuous exercise or heavy lifting for a few days. Pay attention to your body and refrain from overexerting yourself as this could impede your progress or prolong your recuperation.

Continue with your regular skincare routine, but wait until any redness or sensitivity goes away before using severe exfoliation or treatments directly on the treated area. To promote your body's natural processes of fat clearance and metabolism, maintain a healthy lifestyle that includes frequent exercise and a balanced diet. Observe whatever particular guidelines your healthcare practitioner may have given you regarding after-treatment care and activity limitations related to your treatment area and your medical requirements. CoolSculpting or cryolipolysis can help you maximize your recovery and get long-lasting results if you gradually get back to your regular schedule while putting self-care first.

MAINTENANCE OF LONG-TERM RESULTS

Maintaining the shapes and general well-being of your body through healthy lifestyle choices is essential to maintaining the long-term effects of cryolipolysis or CoolSculpting. Even though the treated fat cells are gone forever, it's important to keep your weight constant with regular exercise and a healthy diet to avoid gaining new fat in the areas that haven't been treated. Reduce your intake of processed foods and sugary snacks and increase your intake of fruits, vegetables, whole grains, lean proteins, and whole grains.

To maintain skin elasticity and general hydration levels, stay hydrated by consuming lots of water every day. Build lean muscle mass by incorporating strength training activities into your fitness regimen. This will improve the natural tone and contour of your physique. Keep an eye on how your body reacts to treatments over time, and speak with your doctor if you see any changes or have concerns about maintaining the effects.

ADDITIONAL VISITS AND EVALUATIONS

To guarantee the best possible outcomes and resolve any concerns following CoolSculpting or cryolipolysis therapy, follow-up appointments and evaluations are crucial. Make an appointment for a follow-up visit with your healthcare practitioner so you can assess your progress and talk about any issues or lingering side effects. To monitor changes in the treated region, your provider could take measurements or pictures during these visits.

Talk about any modifications you have made to your lifestyle or health since your therapy, and let us know if you are generally satisfied with the outcome. Your healthcare professional can suggest extra therapies or modifications to your unique response and objectives. It is important to adhere to any customized care instructions given during these appointments to preserve treatment plan continuity and optimize long-term outcomes. You can maintain continuing support and advice from your healthcare physician while reaping the benefits of cryolipolysis or CoolSculpting by being diligent about follow-up appointments and exams.

CHAPTER SEVEN
FAQS & FREQUENTLY ASKED QUESTIONS

DOES COOLSCULPTING CAUSE PAIN?

Cryolipolysis, another name for CoolSculpting, is a non-invasive technique that most patients find to be well-tolerated. You might feel pulling, a little pinching, extreme cold, tingling, numbness, or mild discomfort throughout the procedure. These feelings usually go away in the first five to ten minutes of therapy as the area becomes numb. Without harming the surrounding tissues, the chilling procedure specifically targets and freezes fat cells beneath the skin. In the treated area, this procedure may result in brief redness, swelling, bruising, or skin irritation; however, these side effects normally go away on their own in a few days to weeks.

Your healthcare professional may place a gel pad or a barrier between your skin and the cooling panels to lessen discomfort.

During treatment, patients frequently find the procedure to be pleasant enough to read, use their computers, or even take a nap. To guarantee your comfort and make any necessary setting adjustments, you must let your provider know if you are uncomfortable at any point during the session. Overall, most patients report little to no pain or discomfort following CoolSculpting, making it a well-tolerated therapy.

EXIST ANY HAZARDS CONCERNED?

As long as a licensed healthcare practitioner does CoolSculpting, it is thought to be a safe technique. Nonetheless, there are possible hazards and adverse effects to be mindful of, just like with any cosmetic procedure. Temporary numbness, redness, swelling, bruising, stiffness, tingling, stinging, or mild pains at the treatment site are typical adverse effects. After the treatment, these side effects usually go away on their own in a few days to weeks. More severe adverse effects have occasionally been documented, including paradoxical adipose hyperplasia (PAH), in which there is an increase in fat cells rather than a decrease in the treated area. Although rare, PAH can be addressed with extra treatments.

Before having CoolSculpting, it's important to talk about your expectations and medical history with your provider to make sure you're a good fit and to learn about any possible hazards unique to your case. Your doctor will examine your general health and determine if CoolSculpting is the best course of action for you. To reduce the possibility of issues and maximize your outcomes, they will also provide you with post-treatment care recommendations. CoolSculpting can reduce hazards and produce excellent outcomes if you select a reliable practitioner and adhere to their instructions.

HOW MANY APPOINTMENTS ARE REQUIRED?

The number of CoolSculpting sessions required is determined by a variety of criteria, such as the targeted area or areas, your unique body composition, and the outcomes you hope to achieve. For each treatment area, a CoolSculpting session typically lasts between 35 and 60 minutes. If required, several regions might be treated in a single session. Most patients have noticeable improvements one to three months following their first course of treatment. While some people can get the desired results from a single session, others might need several sessions to reach the best possible body sculpting and fat removal.

To develop a customized treatment plan, your healthcare professional will examine your body and talk with you about your goals during your initial visit. Based on your desired outcome and the amount of fat in the targeted locations, they will propose several treatments. For optimal outcomes, it's critical to adhere to your provider's recommended session intervals and to show up for all scheduled appointments. To sustain your benefits over time, maintenance treatments could be advised. Long-lasting fat reduction and body shaping with CoolSculpting can be attained by following your treatment plan and leading a healthy lifestyle.

CAN SEVERAL AREAS BE TREATED WITH COOLSCULPTING?

The FDA has approved CoolSculpting for the treatment of numerous body parts where hard-to-remove fat typically accumulates. The abdomen, flanks (love handles), thighs, upper arms, double chin, bra fat, back fat, beneath the jawline, and the buttocks are common locations to treat. Because of coolsculpting's adaptability, medical professionals can focus on particular problem areas and tailor treatment regimens to meet the individual body reshaping objectives of each patient.

Different-sized and shaped applicators are used to target different parts of the body during a CoolSculpting session. With the help of controlled cooling provided by these applicators, fat cells are frozen and eventually naturally expelled from the body. Your practitioner will design a customized treatment plan to accomplish the desired body sculpting and fat reduction outcomes, whether you want to target one or many regions. For individuals looking to remove fat in various areas without the downtime associated with invasive treatments, CoolSculpting provides a non-surgical alternative.

WHAT KIND OF OUTCOMES SHOULD I EXPECT?

CoolSculpting offers body sculpting and fat removal with progressive, natural-looking results. After their first session, most patients start to noticeably improve in the regions that have been treated within one to three months. Over several months, the treated area(s) may continue to improve as the body gradually breaks down the frozen fat cells. Results may differ from patient to patient, and some may need more than one session to get the desired effect. It's critical to have reasonable expectations and realize that CoolSculpting targets stubborn fat deposits that are unresponsive to diet and exercise rather than acting as a weight-loss cure.

Following a CoolSculpting procedure, the targeted fat cells are permanently removed from the body. Long-lasting benefits are possible with CoolSculpting as long as you lead a healthy lifestyle that includes regular exercise and a balanced diet. To assist you get the most out of your therapy, your healthcare practitioner will go over reasonable expectations with you and give you post-treatment care recommendations. Through adherence to these rules and scheduled follow-up consultations, as advised, CoolSculpting can provide you with better body shapes and heightened confidence.

CHAPTER EIGHT
IMPROVING OUTCOMES WITH LIFESTYLE MODIFICATIONS
THE SIGNIFICANCE OF EATING WELL

A balanced lifestyle, which is essential for general well-being and continued vitality, is built on the foundation of healthy eating habits. People can make sure their bodies get the vitamins and minerals they need by emphasizing nutrient-dense foods like fruits, vegetables, lean meats, and whole grains. This technique improves energy levels and cognitive function in addition to supporting healthy physical health.

A well-balanced diet high in fiber and antioxidants facilitates better digestion, strengthens the immune system, and increases disease resistance. Additionally, establishing good eating practices lowers the chance of developing chronic illnesses like obesity, diabetes, and heart disease by assisting with weight management.

Meal planning helps incorporate healthy eating into daily living, with an emphasis on moderation and diversity. A varied nutrient intake is ensured by including lean meats and colorful veggies in every meal. Another important factor in maintaining a healthy weight and preventing overeating is portion control.

To further maximize nutrient absorption, stay hydrated throughout the day by drinking lots of water. This will promote metabolism and digestion. People can cultivate long-lasting improvements in their health by progressively adopting these routines.

INCLUDING FREQUENT EXERCISE

Maintaining physical health and improving general well-being requires regular exercise. Exercises that build muscles, increase flexibility, and improve cardiovascular health include jogging, cycling, swimming, and brisk walking. Additionally, these workouts cause endorphins to be released, which improve mood and lower stress levels.

Including a range of exercises guarantees a well-rounded training program that strengthens various muscle groups and increases total endurance. Weightlifting and resistance band workouts are examples of strength training activities that increase muscle mass and support bone density, which are essential for preserving mobility and avoiding injury.

Setting reasonable goals and progressively increasing intensity over time are useful strategies for developing a regular workout regimen. It is best to start with modest exercise and work your way up to more difficult activities to avoid overdoing it and to promote long-lasting fitness routines.

Exercises that correspond with a person's interests increase motivation and satisfaction, which makes it simpler to stick with a long-term commitment. In addition, incorporating regular exercise sessions into daily or weekly schedules guarantees consistency and fosters accountability. People who prioritize regular physical activity report feeling more energized, having better-quality sleep, and being physically resilient overall.

TIPS FOR HYDRATION AND SKIN CARE

It's critical to be properly hydrated to support the health of your skin and your general well-being. Maintaining a healthy body temperature, promoting cellular activity, and eliminating toxins can all be achieved by consuming enough water throughout the day.

Hydrated skin has a more youthful, elastic appearance, which minimizes the visibility of wrinkles and fine lines. Including foods high in water content, such as fruits and vegetables, helps to further promote the hydration of the skin from the inside out. Additionally, the skin retains a healthy moisture barrier and is shielded from environmental damage by utilizing sunscreen and moisturizers.

Gentle cleaning is a key component of effective skin care routines because it removes dirt and pollutants without removing natural oils. Optimal outcomes are ensured by selecting skincare products that are relevant to individual skin types and issues. Frequent exfoliation improves skin luminosity by encouraging cell turnover and removing dead skin cells. Moreover, using serums and creams high in antioxidants promotes the formation of collagen and guards against damage from free radicals. Consistent skin care routines, such as moisturizing and cleaning at night, should be prioritized as they support resilient and healthy skin over time. People can maintain overall skin wellness and attain a hydrated, youthful complexion by implementing these skincare and hydration strategies.

MENTAL HEALTH AND PERCEPTION OF BODY

For general health and self-confidence, it is crucial to support mental wellness and a positive body image. Deep breathing and meditation are two mindfulness practices that lower stress and increase emotional resilience.

Emotional health and self-awareness are improved by partaking in creative and expressive pursuits like art or journaling. Building supportive networks and, when necessary, obtaining professional counseling or therapy offers priceless emotional support and promotes personal development.

Embracing originality and valuing one's special traits and abilities are essential to cultivating a healthy body image. Confidence and self-acceptance are fostered by avoiding comparing oneself to others and concentrating on one's accomplishments. It is better to focus on physical well-being and enjoyment rather than just physical attractiveness when it comes to maintaining a positive relationship with exercise and fitness objectives. Adhering to self-care routines, like getting enough sleep and eating a healthy diet, promotes emotional equilibrium and mental clarity. By placing a high priority on mental health and developing a good body image, people can improve their general well-being and perseverance in the face of adversity.

LONG-TERM WEIGHT LOSS TECHNIQUES

Adopting healthy lifestyle practices that promote long-term success is a necessary step in putting sustainable weight management solutions into practice. Accountability and motivation are increased by setting reasonable goals and regularly monitoring weight and measurements. Healthy weight maintenance is supported by including balanced meals that have an emphasis on nutrient-dense foods and quantity control. Meal preparation at home and planning decrease dependency on processed foods and promote mindful eating practices.

Regular physical activity improves metabolic function and increases calorie expenditure. Examples of this type of physical activity include walking, cycling, and group fitness programs. Consistency and adherence to fitness goals are ensured by finding fun activities that meet personal interests. Emotional eating triggers are decreased and overall well-being is supported by getting enough sleep, practicing stress management, and engaging in hobbies or relaxation techniques. Furthermore, getting advice from medical specialists or registered dietitians offers individualized plans and encouragement for reaching long-term weight control objectives. By using these techniques, people can develop enduring behaviors that support a healthy weight and improve their general well-being.

CHAPTER NINE

FURTHER USES FOR COOLSCULPTING

COOLSCULPTING SUITABLE FOR VARIOUS BODY SHAPES

A non-invasive treatment called CoolSculpting targets fatty deposits that are difficult to lose on different body types. CoolSculpting can be customized to fit various anatomies, regardless of your body's shape—pear, apple, or hourglass. The way the treatment works is that fat cells are frozen and eliminated without causing damage to surrounding tissues thanks to regulated cooling. For instance, by concentrating on the hips and thighs, people with pear-shaped bodies—where fat tends to gather—can gain from CoolSculpting. Similarly, targeted therapies can be used to sculpt and contour the midsection of people with apple-shaped bodies, which are characterized by extra fat around the abdomen.

Knowing your body type is essential to choose which areas to focus on during CoolSculpting treatments.

Physicians evaluate your body shapes to create personalized therapy regimens that target your particular distribution of body fat. CoolSculpting provides a customized approach to fat reduction by focusing on various body types, improving overall body symmetry and proportion. Because each targeted region session lasts approximately one hour, it's perfect for people with hectic schedules who want non-surgical body contouring treatments. The fact that CoolSculpting may be applied to a variety of body shapes highlights how effective it is at reducing specific body fat and improving the appearance of the body.

COMBINING CERTAIN PROCEDURES WITH OTHER TREATMENTS

CoolSculpting can be used in conjunction with other cosmetic treatments to maximize results and treat several aesthetic issues at once. Combining CoolSculpting with procedures like laser therapy for skin tightening or injectable therapies for wrinkle removal is a common combination treatment.

With this method, people can obtain complete body rejuvenation and reshaping in a single session or throughout several sessions. For example, after fat removal, combining CoolSculpting with laser therapy can improve skin tone and elasticity, giving the illusion of more young and sculpted skin.

Combination therapies are customized by clinicians to address the unique objectives and anatomical factors of each patient. CoolSculpting can be used in conjunction with other procedures to provide better body sculpting results that improve skin texture in addition to reducing fat. Because a combination of treatments can produce more significant and all-encompassing aesthetic improvements than a single surgery, this combination is frequently chosen. Combination therapy patients usually have less discomfort and downtime, which makes it a practical choice for people with hectic schedules looking for dramatic cosmetic improvements.

SPECIFICALLY ADDRESSING FAT DEPOSITS

The accuracy of CoolSculpting enables focused treatment of particular fat deposits in different body parts. CoolSculpting can target specific fat pockets, such as love handles, double chins, and thighs, to achieve the desired results.

Applicators made to fit specific body parts enable this tailored approach and provide the best possible outcomes for each treated location. Applicators, for instance, are made to fit a variety of body shapes and sizes, including the abdomen, flanks, inner and outer thighs, arms, and under the chin.

To freeze and eliminate fat cells that are beneath the skin's surface, the applicator is placed over the targeted area during a CoolSculpting session. These treated fat cells are eventually gradually eliminated by the body, giving the area a more sculpted and contoured look. CoolSculpting is a minimally invasive, non-surgical alternative to liposuction by targeting specific fat deposits.

For those looking for localized fat reduction without invasive surgery or lengthy recovery times, this makes it a desirable alternative.

INNOVATIONS IN NON-SURGICAL BODY CONTOURING

Thanks to non-surgical body contouring advancements like CoolSculpting, which provides effective fat reduction without surgery, cosmetic treatments have undergone a revolution. These developments use techniques like cryolipolysis to target and destroy fat cells that are difficult to target while protecting surrounding tissues.

Non-surgical treatments such as CoolSculpting offer a non-invasive alternative with minimum discomfort and downtime, in contrast to traditional liposuction, which requires surgical incisions and recuperation time. They are therefore appropriate for people who want to improve their body contours without having invasive procedures done.

The novel aspect of non-surgical body contouring procedures is its capacity to produce observable reductions in fat using regulated cooling or other cutting-edge technology. Since these procedures are frequently carried out in outpatient settings, patients can quickly return to their regular lives following each session. Through the application of state-of-the-art methods, non-surgical breakthroughs for body shaping are evolving, providing more accessible and safer options than surgical procedures. These developments meet the increasing need for efficient cosmetic procedures that put the convenience and comfort of the patient first.

EXAMINING POTENTIAL ADVANCES IN CRYOLIPOLYSIS

The objective of forthcoming advancements in cryolipolysis is to augment the effectiveness and adaptability of non-invasive fat reduction procedures such as CoolSculpting. To improve patient outcomes, scientists and medical professionals are investigating developments in combination treatments, treatment procedures, and applicator technology. To better target fat cells, for example, ongoing research aims to refine cooling algorithms, guaranteeing consistent and repeatable outcomes across all body types and treatment locations.

Future advancements might also bring new applicator designs that increase the range of treatment possibilities to encompass more difficult or smaller regions. The goal of cryolipolysis's development is to increase the spectrum of cosmetic problems and patient preferences that can be addressed by non-surgical body sculpting. The future of cryolipolysis seems promising for ever more adaptable and efficient fat-loss treatments as technology develops. These advancements highlight the continued dedication to innovation in cosmetic procedures, guaranteeing that patients can obtain cutting-edge choices to meet their preferred aesthetic objectives.

CHAPTER TEN
COST FACTORS AND AVAILABLE FINANCING

COMPREHENDING PRICING STRUCTURES

Cryolipolysis and CoolSculpting cost structures might differ depending on several variables. The areas targeted for fat reduction and the number of treatment cycles required usually determines the cost. Every treatment cycle targets a different body part, such as the thighs or abdomen. The geographic location and standing of the clinic or service provider may also have an impact on prices.

Generally speaking, the price per treatment cycle falls between several hundred and many thousand dollars. It is crucial to speak with several service providers to evaluate costs and guarantee that the contents of each session are transparent. A clinic may provide discounts or package offers for several treatment sessions, which can lower overall expenses.

Knowing how much a treatment will cost includes not just the first sessions but also any follow-up visits or further treatments that might be required to get the desired results. Speaking with providers about price enables people to make informed financial plans and account for any costs related to reaching their body contouring objectives.

VIEWS ON INSURANCE COVERAGE

Insurance usually covers only a portion of cryolipolysis and CoolSculpting operations. Since these surgeries are seen as discretionary cosmetic procedures, most health insurance companies do not cover them. Unless there is a clear medical rationale for fat removal, like lipomas or other medical disorders, insurance providers often do not consider them medically necessary.

People should confirm the specifics of their policy's coverage with their insurance company before making an appointment for a procedure. It's crucial to find out about any possible exclusions or options for coverage that can be applicable in certain medical situations. Patients should often prepare to pay for these therapies out of pocket.

Comprehending insurance coverage insights aids patients in making financial plans for the process and steers clear of unforeseen costs. To help patients manage the cost of treatment, several clinics provide financing options or payment plans.

PLANS FOR FINANCING AVAILABLE

Many clinics provide financing programs to increase accessibility to cryolipolysis and CoolSculpting. With these options, patients can pay for their therapy in installments over time. Medical credit cards, personal loans, or in-house payment plans provided straight by the clinic are examples of financing solutions.

Medical credit cards are a popular option for paying for cosmetic procedures since they sometimes have promotional financing periods that give zero or low interest rates for a predetermined amount of time.

Financial institutions can offer flexible payback terms for personal loans, which can be used to pay for additional sessions or post-procedure care in addition to treatment costs.

Patients can pay for treatment in installments straight to the provider using in-house payment plans provided by clinics. These plans usually don't include a credit check and could provide greater schedule flexibility.

Examining financing options enables people to make an informed decision about a solution that meets their needs both financially and aesthetically, all while staying within their means.

COMPARING THE PRICE OF CONVENTIONAL LIPOSUCTION

It's crucial to weigh the prices of cryolipolysis and CoolSculpting against those of standard liposuction when evaluating body reshaping choices. Conventional liposuction is a surgical technique in which fat cells are suctioned out.

Usually, it is carried out at a hospital or surgical center under general anesthesia.

Traditional liposuction can have a wide range of costs, depending on the region to be treated, the skill of the surgeon, and the type of facility used for the treatment. Because traditional liposuction involves surgery, it is typically more expensive than non-invasive procedures like cryolipolysis and CoolSculpting.

Compared to non-invasive procedures, traditional liposuction may yield more noticeable and quick results, but it also carries greater dangers and requires longer recovery periods.

TIPS FOR BUDGETING TOWARD AFFORDABILITY

Budgeting for cryolipolysis and CoolSculpting requires careful preparation and taking into account several variables. To compare prices, start by finding out what the typical cost of care is in your area and speaking with many providers.

Many clinics provide free consultations during which you can talk about costs and available payment methods without having to commit.

If you plan to have the surgery, think about establishing a savings target and, if necessary, looking into financing possibilities. Treatment costs can be spread out over time and made more affordable every month with the use of personal loans or medical credit cards with promotional financing terms.

Ask about any possible savings options. Some clinics may also provide package offers or discounts for paying for many treatment sessions in advance. Setting up money for prospective maintenance procedures or follow-up visits is also crucial to achieving and sustaining the intended outcomes.

People can efficiently achieve their body sculpting goals and make CoolSculpting and cryolipolysis more inexpensive and accessible by carefully planning their budget and looking into financing options.

CHAPTER ELEVEN
TEACHING PEOPLE ABOUT COOLSCULPTING
PROMOTING A POSITIVE ATTITUDE

Promoting self-acceptance and embracing a variety of body types requires a strong emphasis on body positivity. In the context of CoolSculpting and cryolipolysis, it's critical to stress that the goals of these procedures are about improving a person's comfort and self-confidence rather than meeting social norms for beauty. You can contribute to the debunking of myths and misconceptions about cosmetic operations and body image by teaching others. Urge people to accept their bodies at every stage and to view procedures like CoolSculpting as instruments for raising self-esteem rather than changing intrinsic value.

Emphasize the sense of empowerment that results from making knowledgeable decisions about one's body.

Talk about how CoolSculpting is a non-invasive way to get rid of troublesome fat areas and promote body forms that suit individual objectives. Stress that, despite outside pressures, body positivity is about being at ease and self-assured in one's flesh. In addition to providing CoolSculpting instruction, you enable people to approach cosmetic procedures with a mindset of self-acceptance and love for their bodies.

Give helpful advice on how to include body positivity in regular discussions and interactions on social media. Promote polite conversation regarding body image, emphasizing the process of coming to terms with one's own body rather than striving for perfection. Emphasize how important it is to embrace a range of body types and sizes, demonstrating that there are many different ways to be beautiful. When you promote a body-positive attitude in conversations about CoolSculpting, you make people feel empowered to look into cosmetic procedures while appreciating their attractiveness.

DESCRIBE YOUR OWN EXPERIENCE

Talking about your personal CoolSculpting experiences can be a great approach to inform others and offer firsthand knowledge of the advantages and results of the surgery. Start by explaining how you came to your decision, what made you think of CoolSculpting, and how you investigated the process. Express any early worries or uncertainties you had to show that you are real and relatable throughout your path. Tell us about your consultation experience, including the questions you asked to guarantee a customized treatment plan and the physician you choose.

Describe the actual CoolSculpting process in detail, providing a realistic depiction of what to expect from preparation to recovery. Talk about any pain or other side effects you experienced during the procedure, focusing on how they were handled and the whole experience. Share your timeframe for observing results and offer advice on how to manage swelling or discomfort following therapy. You reassure people thinking about CoolSculpting and provide helpful advice by sharing your own experience.

Invite audience members to ask you questions regarding your CoolSculpting experience to start a conversation. Be open and truthful when addressing typical issues like cost, safety, and efficacy. If at ease, provide before-and-after pictures that showcase the procedure's effects and your metamorphosis. Stress how crucial it is to speak with a professional provider and do much research before having CoolSculpting. You encourage people to think about how CoolSculpting can fit into their own aesthetic objectives and way of life by sharing your journey.

SOURCES FOR ADDITIONAL READING

Having access to trustworthy resources is crucial when investigating CoolSculpting and cryolipolysis to make well-informed judgments. Start by endorsing reliable resources that provide in-depth information on these procedures, such as peer-reviewed papers, medical journals, and recognized healthcare websites. Emphasize the advantages of comprehending the science of CoolSculpting, particularly how targeted and removed fat cells are achieved with controlled cooling technology. Provide references to research on patient outcomes, safety procedures, and long-term effects of CoolSculpting.

Encourage looking into the educational resources offered by licensed CoolSculpting practitioners, including fact sheets, patient endorsements, and online consultations. These resources can provide information on available treatments, anticipated outcomes, and individualized care plans catered to each patient's needs. Urge people to consult with licensed medical specialists, such as plastic surgeons and dermatologists who specialize in CoolSculpting procedures, for advice. You give people the ability to confidently manage their CoolSculpting journey by providing them with extensive information.

Talk about how important it is to look through patient testimonials and before-and-after pictures when looking for CoolSculpting providers. These graphic aids help illustrate the possible results of treatment and set reasonable expectations. Urge people to join educational webinars or seminars held by CoolSculpting specialists so they may learn more about the advantages of the process and ask questions. By pointing people in the direction of trustworthy sources, you assist them in their quest for knowledge and help them make informed decisions about CoolSculpting.

RAISING AWARENESS IN YOUR NEIGHBORHOOD

CoolSculpting and cryolipolysis are procedures that should be discussed openly and truthfully to raise awareness in your community. Start by discussing the advantages of CoolSculpting as a non-invasive body sculpting alternative with friends, family, and coworkers.

Talk about common misconceptions and explain how controlled cooling technology, used in CoolSculpting, safely targets and eliminates fat cells that are resistant to reduction.

Plan informative workshops or events in your town. Collaborate with wellness centers or healthcare providers to host talks about CoolSculpting. Ask qualified experts to talk about the procedure's science, patient eligibility requirements, and possible outcomes. Give participants the chance to learn directly from professionals in cosmetic treatments and ask questions. You may foster a welcoming atmosphere where community members can explore their interest in CoolSculpting by organizing these events.

Use social media to spread the word about CoolSculpting by posting educational articles, videos, and user reviews that emphasize the procedure's advantages and results. Encourage others to participate in conversations by asking questions or offering their opinions on topics like body confidence and aesthetic objectives. Partner with bloggers or influencers who have had CoolSculpting procedures to help them share their experiences and reach a larger audience. You may positively influence the conversation around body positivity and the options available for boosting self-confidence through cosmetic treatments by actively raising awareness in your community.

HELPING OTHERS WITH THEIR COOLSCULPTING EXPERIENCES

Offering support to others during their CoolSculpting journey entails offering words of wisdom, direction, and encouragement. As they explore their options for body contouring cosmetic surgery, start by attentively listening to their worries and inquiries regarding CoolSculpting and extending empathy and compassion. Talk about your personal experience or understanding of the process, clearing up any common misunderstandings and offering comfort based on your unique perspective.

Encourage people to look up CoolSculpting providers and make appointments with licensed experts who focus on aesthetic procedures. Provide advice on how to formulate questions for consultations, stressing the significance of going over treatment areas, anticipated outcomes, and possible side effects. To help them better understand the results and aesthetic changes of CoolSculpting, encourage them to go at before-and-after pictures and patient testimonies.

During the healing phase, continue to assist the patient and give helpful advice on how to handle any discomfort or swelling that may arise after treatment. Talk about self-care techniques including drinking enough of water, giving yourself a light massage, and adhering to the suggested amount of physical activity. When you visit people having CoolSculpting, make sure to offer support and acknowledge their accomplishments as they move closer to reaching their ideal body shapes.

www.ingramcontent.com/pod-product-compliance
Lightning Source LLC
Chambersburg PA
CBHW071838210526
45479CB00001B/186